'WATER RISING'

Printed for Major Jack Moore TD

Index of fi

Still, and the
time atom shall
be again,
keeping
unhurried clarity
of people,
and the
translucent
hands of pink
crabs,
shall play with
the water children.

They are like fountains
their talk sparkles
patters quickly as falling water.
Their talk is a never ending circle
as in a fountain
water seems a never ending stream.
Yet is the same
as that which but a while ago
spilt forth in brilliance and died.

Keep smiling always
the chirruping
birds
have pleasured the summer
time enough to cry
when
time
has gone
by the sea soft singing
I hear
gleaming
teeth happy laughing sounds
of dishes
stacked
and
drip drying.

The child has gone
now the day is old
and callused by many hands.
The child has gone
so the taste of wood smoke
assumes new poignancy.
The child has gone
her name waits in ambush
behind the laughter of sparrows.

Sunblinded
sandbedded
somniferous sea soft whispered
sun worshipers lie

Sunblinded
pebble blistered
peace of mind from ears transistored
we pass them by

Sunpounded
sand sinking
sea somnambulant starfish clustered
sun worshipers lie.

Moving and thrusting without direction or
sentient action, waters of the wild
mountain, belying your strength with sweet
singing.
Rush upon me delirium and wayward
wondering, seeking to know the source
of your power, being exorcised of
longing.
Seeming to sing only to stones
buried in embraces, comforted, soft rushing
bursting into myriads of water-wild
flowers.
Run through the ribs of sheep long dead as
I stumble upon remains that keep
sanctified and lonely, weathered splinters
of bone.

The time of the dragon
has come
and with it that
bending of the
mind,
that talking
smoke of accident
made purposeful
malevolent,
the time has come
unheralded
and now it sings
in bolts of
brass,
the creeping points
of knife blades
shine,
to join the joy
of bottle caps.
The time of the dragon
has come
and with it that
bending of the
mind,
that shifting sand
of sad sequence
predestined by no
sanity,
the time has come
unheralded
but now its coming
can be seen,
with failing strength
of self regard
the powerless thought
capitulates.

I am a line
bounding
areas can be sublime
essential information
is
restricted to the gathering
planes,
I am a line
envelop
the instant and complex
forms I cannot,
one day I shall become
a sphere
a volume grandiloquent
fat
and all the lines
both far and near
will wonder what I'm
dreaming at.

Hoe the cotton edge
while hormone spray
at work within,
locusts cast fat shadows
now are thin,
lie like a bird in fine
red dust
fly wide in the sun
and take your rest.
Hoe the cotton edge
and keeping tender
neck
salt pickled black
without a hat
many singing-wings
will creep and hide,
small ants
dispose of those
that linger, in this heat
a man needs cotton pants.
Hoe the cotton edge
declining sun is etching
hills,
hear in the evening time
the bitter guns.

Temperate
breeze of England's Spring
remind me of my Cretan
days,
Woods
slow and torpid cling
to full desire of Summer
sun,
Come
suffer no regret
expunge the trace of resined joys
begun,
Innocent
comradeship of hands
entangled in grapes of gold and
green,
Remembering
pays tribute to our feet
that ache and joy we two
again.

Pursue the half remembered kisses
sweet as razored cheeks,
delivered of static electricity
perturbation and release.
Erect a dream which soothes
the edge of memory
sharp as a fir-cone in the fire
a nail broken to the quick.
Sweet and fey as Victorian boots
is there a miniature dog
neat as a cat beneath the potted
plant?
Cameo, I was frightened as a child
by she who knew me then spoke
disguised, being confused I caught a bus
wasting, in retrospect, a hope.
Beat the drum, but muted, exorcise
the ghosts of paths that twine
with daisies, and fields that grow
cow muck between my toes.
Walk with me again on dry cement
or in the rain
listen to the talk of worlds or windows
remind me of my childhood days.

Mist and gold become the mountain
and each fold
can hide the silent stream
that sings from hand to hand
unseen.

Clouds that touch each peak of stone
they speak to much
and following the lilac line
of streams gone dry, whisper passing of
the time.

Summers come and velvet moss grows
black upon the sun
then in between soft rain
comes marching feet, that meet
we two again.

Walking in the skies bird's song
says that sweet sun dies,
and sheep people the twilight ground
coming soft the
valley sound.

Fit into this place the sum of silence
in your face
talking with each pampered tip, a separate voice
of fingers smooth
my lip.

Bend the cold wind, be simple with each rope
and fold, now tented sleep shall dream
until the sun's dance
in your eyes
can green.

Morning rain comes melting distant hills
I lift my pain
and taking soft the muddy track
without a word from loving stones
I'm going back.

Lime that grew before you
knew the fat mud
splash beneath your
feet.
Come to me in later years
be contoured hills
in soft retreat.
Searching crisp and subtle
risk the blade that cuts
skin deep into
the wood.
Flakes your ribs and keeping
kids happy as sand
and children
could.
Pick up the flakes
which make a drifting dune
Or, sweep the notes that
weep from sharpened
eyes and broadcast through
an open door.

Simple day
of bread and cheese
skies of blue and seedless
clouds,
comes a memory of things
patchwork dresses
on the ground.
Beads of glass
and shading walls
under arch and silent
stone,
pick a hand and playing
King, make a servant
of the time.
Kind of sun
and ancient flies
coffee cooling into
grains,
carry back to England's
Spring, all the buttons
here in Spain.

Do not sing
romantic songs
about a union that came
to middle age
a bit too soon
did not sink
into the ease
of times remembered, and reminisce
from time to time
a kiss,
perhaps we were
spared the sad
remarks
whatever did I
see
in her, in him
and as my lazy
memory
grows dim
I shalln't remember
what was so dear
then, even onions
produce a tear,
so sing me no
romantic songs
and say
goodbye to blooming flowers
within, for after all
the song was growing thin
and maybe
in another life
we ran away
to Spain
or maybe
it was just the rice
that clutters up
my drain,
in any case
you break things
which
I never could abide
how is it now
I miss you
and have no car to ride.

Sweep
the gardens of your mind
where grow the weeds
of glass
Keep
in memory of mine
the bitter herbs that
summers pass
Seek
the grounded stones
that once on air
could dance
Weep
for sounds of autumn
winds and smell the ash
of grass
Then
until the spring has
come and peopled into
may
Count
the dunes and solitude
has heaped so long
the day.

Dolphins tail first through
the sun
breaking waves
across my mind
for fun,
Chicken playing the green
sea foam
through the hair
waters sing
of home,
Wings of salt wind
pregnant
to the skies tup
bars that rope
me to each
quadrant,
Come you bitch
and plane
each wave will
have us, loose
then come again.

Lap of sea refracted
by grey stone
rocks the mind within
and grey the skies
remind me of my home,
Shaped by hands of men
long gone
now brushed by seagulls
hardened cries
and wind alone,
I hear you wind as in
my mast you moan
lick the wires
and tongue the sea to
twilight chrome.

Sing lament of walls
then bring cement and sand
barrow concrete
and take away
the spoil,
trim lines that sag
and mind not
the calloused thumb
worms dig a tomb
within the soil,
Summers gone
and bricks shall deck
in soft green mould
and petals settle
in the sun,
Then shall the winter mind remember
splinters lodged beneath the nail
all those deeds we can dismember
better had they been
undone.

Ice axe mud
from bitter wind
has turned
Trod by hooves
into a
cratered land
Claws of grass
withdraw into
a sheath
Frozen nails
step softly
all around
Sunrise creeps
the shadows
to their holes
Nodding heads
set in a
ragged line
Time to seek
the welcome sound
of man
Dusty hay
upon the
pitted ground.

After rain came
the odour of colour,
stop every step
to taste
grit on
the ground.
Washed to an edge
each smell
has a brother,
can it be seen
each colour
a sound.

Five woods to pass
and come at last, to a tranquil place
where sheltered waters dwell
to rest a while
and run with style, through roots
of oyster shell.
Five woods in all
the cold winds call, and rush
from tip to tip
of trees that mass each flank
and steepened bank, or hug
the rivers lip.
Five woods we met
best not forget, the buoyant arms
that hold us near
then slide with grace
at a walking pace, once more
into the lilting mere.

No tears for hills
teeth white stones
and dust bent shade
Flies intimate with legs
carved brown and gold
detach upon a breeze,
cool the sound of sea lips
pound and mumble
through hot stubble,
Donkey-black bent women work
the fields and follow after
men into the pillared haze.

Cold nights of starshine
give me a pain
neck stiff with gazing
or whiplash remain.

Better a duvet
and warm toasted feet
now that the river
has strengthened its beat.

Do we fork left
or do we fork right
now that the river
has come into night.

Whatever direction
had better be quick
the tide is a running
the black mud is thick.

Starshine and moonshine
warm hands and hips
swift talking wavelets
and slow walking lips.

Two merry people plait
times slippery thread
silently singing
and longing to bed.

Soft comes the morning
responsible light
now we are thinking
that others are right.

Outside of the river
the broken seas roar
rolling and plunging
upon a lee shore.

If we are dauntless
intrepid and brave
fair winds will lift us
while others may rave.

Romy

Hide the message on your brow
write invisible
as ink,
till children hold the paper
to a fire
and heat,
reveals each word
in neat
calligraphy.

A sign that says its "open door"
to cranks and crazies
welcomed in,
can be confusing to a herd
of wildebeest
or even men,
and leave them standing hypnotised
in the headlamps
of your eyes.

Time to step on the moving road
untie the ropes
farewell the quay,
the wind is calling warm, so rich
a dish to dine without
parsimony,
tomorrow brings its hills to climb
and will not wait too long
for you or me.

CAT

Feet of friendly crows, that flocked
and yomped about your eyes,
have given you a pensive look
your forehead in repose.
Do not fret my dearest cat
or shun the morning light,
for nothing but the tranquil night
has trespassed on your nose.

Maybe the silent S.A.S, have stalked
with bootblack toes upon your spine,
their footsteps linger even yet
and match my fingers fond caress.
Now, in the hush of evening
you hunt upon the land,
the small and crippled animals
your appetites possess.

Your secret smile, becomes a purr
your neck will arch to greet my hand
when cryptic light meets
fairy sea, we'll pause in wonder for a while.
You thought you were a silkie once
while really you were just a cat,
with spotted coat and curling tail
what innocents those claws defile.

Do not eat me little one
do not bite the sailors hand that pats,
but curl up-soft upon my chest and
dream of quick and juicy rats.

Rag Doll

Brown is not my favourite word
Melanin skin, tanned and sleek
Should have a phrase more subtle
Yet in a week
Without circuitous and irritating talk
"Do you see?" (of course I do) it's time to seek
Another way to meet with you.

When the Puppet-Master cut
The strings, and tumbled you in a heap
Rag doll, helpless, abandoned
And for a moment, meek
I tripped on tabs of innocence
And found no words
To freely speak.

Do not kick the light bulb
Hanging high by its twisted thread
Nor rail against your Mother
Or wish the day, so soon, to bed
But rather sit in silence, a smile upon your cheek
And sip the red Italian wine
While music sings a soft, and tawny beat.

Woodsmoke

Sitting now in the woodsmoke
of my afternoon
sipping coffee black
and rich,
I see the ghosts of future hours
that leave their imprint
on the day.

Home, with greystone hearth
and favourite stick
a dog, his chin
upon my feet,
the warmth of fire to ease
my bones, a kettle singing
on the stones.

Or drinking in the open square
at tables full of careless young,
scattered near and far, their
packs,
with labels strange
and casual
style.

A vision, full of ethnic dreams
where mountains sink
beneath
the moon,
and standard issue
maidens glide, to welcome
sailors from the sea.

Savour the delicate ghosts of days
set against a velcro sky
each hour will drift
into a mound,
like autumn leaves, collect
and spread their bounty on
the fertile ground.

Night Passage

Listen to the engine beat, whisper of the wake
strain the eye and black of night
deny, a vision of the sea or sky.

Rush with sail aloft to catch each breath,
the creak of rope and block, all other sounds
disguise, except the angry rock and waves demise.

Blinded by the rain, mesmerised by lights
seen red or green, sometimes they fade
yet seem, to guide us through an endless shade.

Dawn shall come, and sleeping gulls arise
take wing, to skim the waves and
bring, a message to the naked land.

Pity the Landsman in his crumpled bed
of down, he does not know the nature of the
sound, that freshly minted sky and sea, compound.

A brief affair

You waved, out of the window of your car
I caught the gesture, from afar
feet rooted to the spot, my hand replied
sad without your touch or voice
my eyes, they cried.

The train was two hours late
death on the line, they said
they gave us coffee, free
to pass the time
within my mind, I stroked your knee.

Out of the window of your car
you waved
I caught the picture, much too far
feet rooted to the spot, my hand replied
anticipating loss
my eyes, they cried.

Be Still

Is that a smile which hides
a drooping line of dialogue
plunging in the sadness of your mouth?

Take me by a hand who's fingers twist
like sea-anemones, through rings of silver
and trace eclectic paths of passion on my skin.

Whisper to me in the night, or
swim, within your belly and pulse
like a squid among the falling hours.

Where is your daytime ocean of
desire, hidden in a press of traffic
motorway maps printed on the inside of your eyes?

See the looping roads describing secret valleys
rounded hills like ice-cream, licked
by English tourist tongues.

Give me a moment of your time
be still, listen to the moorland Lark
calling insensate to the sky.

New Forest

There were Horses in the night
wild, not domesticated
running free
you trusted me
as I slept and you were awake
for I was there, only
a breath away.

The noises they made contrasted
soft clipping of grass
loud snapping of sticks
such a mix
under the trees where our tent
a thin film of privacy
sheltered us from their sight.

They cried out to each other
wildly they ran
through the dark
the forest park
where campers came and made
civilised clusters around their cars
in the full light of day.

How come?

A scar on my arm shows up
white against my tan
what is odd, at fifty eight
is that I don't recall the event
but that my skin remembers.

There is one on my leg
that sits like a trilobite in stone
the memory of that is clear.

Under the table-cloth, hanging low
the Court Marshal was short
the creatures crimes were not denied
verdict, death by Daddies knife.

The unfaithful Panda dodged
the knife skipped into my flesh
when I was four.

At that age one lacks the skill in
Panda slaying that later experience
provides.

Bleak Haven

Bring me the tree-stumps of desire
Pulled by the dentist wind
Cut me the kindling of remorse
To fire my summer down.

Rip up the hedgerows of my dreams
Sheltering the frosted web
Cover the place with vivid green
Yellow unsightly flowers of rape.

Palimpsest of reputation
Rectitude and salutation
Stroking a complacent cat.

There is another land it seems
Where hedgerows are again full grown
Tree-roots revel in the earth
And flowers grow beside quiet streams.

Coppiced limbs with new made buds
Hide webs dew-decked upon each dawn
And yellow is a colour we love
Of buttercup and dandelion.

After Elizabeth BB

How do I love you? Let me count the ways.
I love you as the horses love the sun
Turning to its heat after long cold night
Steam, rising from flanks dew-wet
When morning time has just begun

I love you like the aftermath of rain
Sweetening the summer day
Each drop is sucked deep, into soil
Each leaf reluctant to let fall
Scent of brick and new laid dust
Dawdle in the lazy air
Drying deltas trouble ants
That forage, busy everywhere

I love you as the kestrel loves the wind
Hanging on liquid air
Her slender shadow grazes reeds, she
Stoops, before the vole can know,
Rips out the heart and lays it bare

I love you as the horizon loves the hills
Crisp in autumn light
The frost still clings to every stalk and leaf
Except where sun has licked the edge
With innocent delight.

The Homecoming

The three sharp prows turn toward the sun
Dancing in the waves, the dolphin play
Wild clouds run before the wind
Rigging whines with joy
Foam boils from a triple wake
Land is fading into grey.

Blind to the hearth-fires burning bright
In the eyes of wives or lovers
Deaf to their cries and tears in the night
The sea is calling fierce and true
Day is breaking without care.

Years are gone, smoothed like stones
Ground beneath the ice
When heroes come, home to ash
Cold as a winter moon
Their eyes are dead
Hands and faces dark with distance
Keels have kissed the beach at last.

Where have the wives and lovers passed
With rounded limbs and joyful laughter
No echoes ring through the ancient house
Blackened beams and crippled walls
Mice nest where once the people danced
No more, a fiddle's wild enchanted singing
Crows toss in a fretful wind or
Strut upon the broken tiles.

Three sharp prows turn toward the sun
Where dancing dolphin play and wild clouds run
Rigging whines with joy, foam boils up once more
The sea is calling fierce and true
Day is breaking without care.

Flat Land

Three horses ran
They were having fun
Galloping through the tall grass
Spray flying from shallow pools

Late afternoon sun
Making rainbows as they ran
Shining clean and low
Under isolated clouds

Land, flat to the horizon
Sharp and severe
Nothing grows but scrub trees
And clumps of horses

Waterlogged fields
Hedges and ditches
Keep them apart, but they cry
And shout across the miles

After you had gone
They ran through the fields
In that clear light
As if they were free.

Three horses ran
Late afternoon sun
Land, flat to the horizon
After you had gone.

22nd November

Four generations in the room
the eldest like the youngest
not so sure upon his feet
the other two not yet accustomed
to their roles tripping over words
and phrases.

Eighty two years they span
who is the granddad now
men who think and look
unlike yet share a common
thread and all of them alive
today this month of '98

Take the photos of this manly
dance around the furniture and
in and out "door" one says the other
"light" a third says "tea?"
"no milk thanks" says the third daddy
 the eldest now is eighty three.

Look into the eyes of each and you
might see a picture of a perfect son
and looking back the other way a father
who has stood against the odds
and will again until the time has come
when three much older men are
waiting for another one.

More fun with Two

Grin to grin the couple lay
clothes upon the floor
windows open to the day
gravel drives
standing guard like geese
ever-ready to alarm
each innocent car or tread.

Silver hair and double chin
belly to belly and eye to eye
she and him
while books in tottering piles
waited their turn and number
some had two but no one knew
or cared.

Later in a narrow bath
accommodating bodies sat
proving anew
what Archimedes had defined
was he alone that clever Greek
or did he seek
that same accord entwined?

Oh Dear!

Never tell me what to do;
when I was very young
I knew that such behaviour
is ill-bred, dominion, holding low
esteem, having no ear to hear
a word that's said.

From which false page
did you take advice
the hauteur ill becomes your face
promoting rage without
a change of pace
lacks craft and subtle wit.

Do not tell me it's a joke;
I hear the threat behind
the cloak of brittle repartee,
that easy order once released
can never be constrained
within the forms of etiquette.

A dog will love you
when it learns to come
then nuzzle the hand that feeds
and grooms, conditioned reflex
in a pet is good
but in a man, no fun.

Circle

Two boys cycle
through a puddle
drawing wet tyre-circles
on dry tarmac.

Paths drawn with water
and concentration
through the long afternoon
into evening.

WATER RISING.

Their houses were separate.
He lived on a hill in his boat.
When the wind howled through the rigging-wires
the mast transmitted its oscillation to the boat below
and he was rocked to sleep.
She lived in a big house.
The many rooms rang with the laughter of her friends,
but he was not invited.
They had made a mistake
It was mutual.
It was a big grand wonderfully insane mistake
they had made, becoming lovers.

Slowly the waters grew deeper.
Her house was inundated.
She searched in all the familiar places for dry ground.

Houses were not difficult to find.
At each location she could see the waters were rising
threatening to engulf her life.
She fled to the next place, but it was the same.
Not one of her friends could understand her hesitation.
She had money enough to buy a new home.
They could not see the water.

The evening breeze would bring the sodden remnants
of household furniture, drifting half submerged
like the drowned and bloated bodies of sheep.
Sometimes these things would bump together,
as if trying to re-create their previous relationship.
In the morning they would be gone.

Slowly the landscape changed.
Nothing was simple any more.
Straight lines vanished and paths became sinuous,
routine tasks circuitous.
She began to hide her activities from her friends.
She was lonely but no longer alone.

The world looked different, elongated and reflected
but restless, trembling to every cats-paw of wind.
She visited the hill more and more often.
When the water reached the boat it would float
and join it's natural environment once again.
It was alive, graceful, ready to escape the confines
of the land.

Then he would be gone.

On the hill the world was simple.

The waters rose and fell in response to the sun and moon.
A skylark filled the air in the hush of evening,
causing her to weep tears of joy.
Young rabbits came out of the brambles to graze.
They were unafraid, she was terrified.

The season changed.

The first frosts nipped at the leaves and crisped the dew,
a fresh wind curled delicately around drainpipes, rude
with icicle tongues and children slid on ice-covered puddles
with screams of joy.
Thin columns of smoke climbed effortlessly
into the cloudless sky and a pale sun blazed low on the horizon,
reflecting into grateful eyes.
Gravel crunched underfoot and white breath hung in the air.
Old acquaintances met by chance and remembering good times,
arranged to meet again.

New plans were made, old ones resurrected.
There was movement and purpose in her life.

The water was no longer rising.

Now he lived alone on his boat.
When the wind howled through the rigging-wires,
the mast transmitted its oscillation to the ice-locked hull below
keeping him awake.

RED DOG

Red dog run
fetch the toy sheep
skid on the tiles
and jump with grace
to tongue my cheek.

Red dog leap
to greet me home
such joy gives me
pause to ask a question,
why do I roam?

One Act Play

It is the same each day, the bar staff
have a rota
but you and me we drink and speak
our lines
oft-times
each and every night without remit
or time off for good behaviour.

Astrology

How many days are there in each month
the calendar says it seldom changes
what a lie
we know they multiply
now you are away
each day
will be a drag.

Take for example monday
which they say follows sunday
what a cheek
to start the week
in such a way
some celestial dramatist is in the pay
of a tabloid rag.

He says my life is good, my sign is full of
benefit and joy, he cannot know
unless he's cruel
how much I miss you
in the month of May
perhaps he misconstrued
or lost a day?

Burnt Sugar

Burnt sugar in a voice
Grown far from the mists of home
What strange fruit is eaten there
In a land trod smooth by time.

Salt-flats blinding in a midday sun
Where buzzards walk and bushes roam
Hot rubber in the afternoon
Your eyes are green, your skin is brown.

Lift your arms into the air
Twist and stretch to itch the bone
Stones are hot beneath the feet
Dance to the beat of a silent tune.

ADVICE TO SAILORS

Do not risk the fickle winds of doubt
Or heel to summer squalls of praise
But keep your course and if you must
Use the friendly breeze of lust!

Avoid the over-falls of fear
Do not heed the smiling lights of town
Keep your course and you can trust
The friendly sailing breeze of lust!

In a moonless black confusing night
Look out for half-tide rocks of pain
If your compass maybe wrong or bust
There's just the sailing breeze of lust!

Dear sailors heed me one more time
Please memorize this sage advice
When at last your pen begins to rust
Seek the friendly breeze of lust!

SEA LOVER

Pale ghost in the night gleam
Of uncurtained windows
The point of your breast swings
Arcs of navigation, your thighs
Reflect the sea swell in my blood.

Outside the taste of silence
A night Owl woodwinds the valley
Dusting the slope stacked cottages
For prey, you move softly
To devour my sleep.

Blackbird scolding the morning
Pink and grey and Venus fading
Sea, distantly breathing
On the shore, like a mouse
You snore, sweetly.

Invitation

Come with me and see the world, painted afresh
each dawn, watch the horizon define its self from scented air
the sea warm, like a duvet on which we rest.
Come with me and be the best you can

Leave the past upon the compost heap
Let it rot as nature intended, becoming rich and fertile
wisdom where new life grows.
Open your eyes innocent of expectation
look for the real; wet decks fair winds, dry decks harsh.
Smile at the world with me, be passionate and bold

We are not yet too old
Come with me and find the mystery, of what you want to be
So, when in years to come a child with school books says
 "it's boring, listing all those rocks," you say.
"Ah! But there is where I found my magic pearl
and heard the sound of mermaids washing socks".

Bank Holiday Monday

Woodworm in the stair-tread
Loci more numerous than the
Milky-way, illuminating solstice night
Rubber gloved and booted
You dress in favourite 'worky' clothes
Sander at the ready to expose
A galaxy of holes
Middle class gods demand a
Bare-faced sacrifice
I fear the night
In case, by some malicious oversight
The sky is neat, scrubbed smooth by
Latex covered hands and booted feet

KEMNAY May 6th 2020

Silence, stretched with finches
Crow speak and distant buzzard call
Sun warmed seat to ease a
Hip, soured by winters teases
Solitary bees, rampant grouse
In the background a granite house
Dogs leap conformist picket
Washing dances pink and blue
Blackbird challenges the garden
Sweet a custard from a spoon

May wind, warm and full of swallows
Butterflies, like apple blossom
Flit the Beech, decked frogspawn green
Hunting the scent of cabbages.

Printed in Great Britain
by Amazon